The Care and Maintenance of the
REDFOOT TORTOISE
Geochelone Carbonaria
in Captivity

By Mike Pingleton

Carapace Press
London

THE CARE & MAINTENANCE OF THE REDFOOT TORTOISE
GEOCHELONE CARBONARIA IN CAPTIVITY

Text © 2001 Mike Pingleton
Photographs © 2001 Mike Pingleton and A. C. Highfield
All rights reserved

This edition first published 2001

ISBN 1 873943 90 3

**Published and distributed by
Carapace Press UK and USA**

Visit our website for latest titles

www.vidi-herp.com
www.carapacepress.com

For additional information on tortoise and turtle care please visit the Tortoise Trust website at
www.tortoisetrust.org

Or write:
**Tortoise Trust
BM Tortoise
London
WC1N 3XX
England**

The Care of Redfoot Tortoises in Captivity

Redfoot tortoises make wonderful pets that you can enjoy for a lifetime. They are intelligent animals, each with a distinctive personality. Redfoot tortoises thrive in captivity, if provided with all of the necessary requirements - proper diet, environment, enclosures, and so on. This book attempts to address each element of captive care, and is based on the observations and experiences of tortoise owners, scientists, and zookeepers worldwide. Redfoot tortoises are being bred in captivity in increasing numbers. They are one of the more popular tortoises, and yet there is much we don't know about them, including many details of their natural history. Like most animals, each question answered results in still more questions!

Natural History Notes

The Redfoot Tortoise occurs throughout much of tropical South America. It ranges from Panama and Colombia east through Venezuela all the way to the Atlantic, then down through Brazil, Bolivia, Paraguay, and northern Argentina. It is found on Trinidad, and has been introduced to many islands in the West Indies. The Redfoot occupies a number of habitats within this extensive range. It occurs in all types of forest habitat (rainforest, temperate forest, and dry thorn forest), and also dwells in savanna areas, including man-made grasslands resulting from ranching and slash-and-burn agricultural practices. Forest edges and savannas seem to be the preferred habitat for this species.

Coloration varies somewhat throughout the range, but the typical Redfoot has a black or dark brown carapace, with a small yellow spot in the center of each scute. The plastron is usually a light horn color, sometimes with darker reddish brown patterns along scute sutures. The head and lower jaw typically have yellow markings, and the limbs and tails have scales marked with red.

The carapaces of Redfoot tortoises from Colombia and Panama are a grey or dark brown, with yellow and orange markings on the head and limbs. In the Amazon Basin, the carapace is black or dark brown, and the head and limb markings range from yellow to orange to red, or any combination of the three. In some parts of northern Argentina and Paraguay, a smaller form of Redfoot occurs, with head and limbs marked with a deep scarlet. These are known as "Cherry Heads" and are quite popular among tortoise keepers, but are available in smaller numbers (and so are more expensive!)

The carapaces of many adult male Redfoot tortoises are slightly pinched in the middle, giving them a waist of sorts. When viewed from above, they somewhat resemble a peanut. No explanation exists for this physical feature, which is found predominantly in males - females are usually a bit wider at mid-body. Adult males average about twelve inches (30 cm), and females are typically a few inches smaller. The record length is just over seventeen inches (43 cm). Males can easily reach twenty pounds (9 kg) or more, while females weigh a bit less. The oldest living Redfoot on record lived fifty six years, and thirty to forty year old tortoises are not uncommon. Sexual maturity is usually reached between eight and twelve years of age.

Redfoot tortoises are closely related to the Yellowfoot tortoise, *Geochelone denticulata*. They share much of the same range, but not the same habitat, avoiding competition for resources. Yellowfoots are forest dwelling tortoises, and avoid the open, drier savannas and forest-edge habitats preferred by Redfoot tortoises. In turn, Redfoot tortoises are not usually found in forest areas where denticulata are present. The two closely related species are not known to interbreed, even in captivity; the courtship rituals of each species are unique. The differences in habitat and courtship rituals are probably important isolation mechanisms, keeping the two species separate. They are thought to share a common ancestor, *Geochelone hesterna* from the late Miocene of Colombia.

Redfoot tortoises spend the daylight hours foraging for fallen fruit, flowers, grasses, succulents, fungi, and leaves. They are omnivorous, eating insects and other invertebrates, and carrion. Like many other tortoise species, they are known to gnaw on bones, presumably for the calcium and other minerals they contain. Much like North American box turtles, hatchling and juvenile Redfoot tortoises live hidden among dead leaves and grass, and are seldom seen until they attain some size.

Redfoot tortoises are fairly intelligent, as tortoises go, and quickly learn to recognize their keepers. They can apparently see a range of colors; I feed my Redfoot tortoises on red plastic plates every time, and without a doubt they react differently to a red plate than to one of another color! Their sense of smell is developed enough to aid them in finding their favorite food in a pile of fruits and vegetables. Many keepers say their Redfoot tortoises seem to enjoy a scratch of the head or chin, and they are known to follow their owners around, and to take food from fingers. Personalities vary - some are shy and retiring, others are more outgoing and inquisitive. Adults do not grow so large that they cannot be kept indoors, another reason why they make good pets. Since they are long-lived, you can look forward to a life-long relationship with your Redfoot!

Captive Care

Redfoot tortoises live in forest and savanna areas of tropical South America, where temperature ranges are fairly constant year-round. They live and thrive in a warm, humid environment, with some fluctuations provided by dry and rainy seasons. In this stable climate, they rarely need to endure extreme high or low temperatures. Emulating this environment for your captive Redfoot is not as difficult as you might think; it won't be necessary to recreate Brazil within your entire dwelling - just a small area! Here are the basic elements you will need to provide:

- Daytime temperatures of 84-92°F (29-33°C), no higher than 94°F (34°C)
- Nighttime temperatures no lower than 70°F (21°C)
- As much natural sunlight as possible
- A regular 12 - 14 hour photoperiod
- Variable temperatures within the enclosure (thermal gradient)
- Humidity levels between 60 and 80 percent in the enclosure
- Plenty of fresh water every day
- A varied, healthy diet
- Hide boxes to sleep in at night
- Sunny spots to bask, plenty of shade
- Room for exercise

It may seem like a lot of things to consider, but Redfoot tortoises really are not much more trouble than a dog or cat, once basic care routines are established. They even have a few advantages over felines and canines - they won't claw up the furniture, and they don't bark to be let out at 3AM!

Choosing a Tortoise

There are a few things to consider when it is time to pick out a Redfoot. It goes without saying, of course, that you'll want a healthy animal, and that is your first concern. There are kind souls out there who have taken in ill or severely debilitated tortoises, who have nursed them back to health and given them a good home, but if this is your first tortoise, you may want to start off with a healthy specimen.

Captive Bred or Wild Caught?
There are a lot of Redfoot tortoises in captivity. How many more need to be imported? Some people would argue that buying wild caught animals supports the import trade and diminishes tortoise populations in the wild. If you want adult Redfoot tortoises, chances are you may have to purchase WC imports, which can be problematic. WC tortoises usually harbor internal and external parasites, and may have respiratory infections and other problems associated with capture and importation stresses.

Be prepared to have WC tortoises examined by a veterinarian and treated for any number of problems. If possible, purchase established tortoises that have already cleared of any health risks. If you prefer to 'grow your own', then captive bred Redfoot tortoises are the way to go. They generally have few of the problems associated with wild caught tortoises, but should still be closely examined by you and your veterinarian.

Where to Buy?
Many people buy their first Redfoot from a pet shop. Their experiences range from the sublime to horrific. Get more information while you consider your purchase - what kind of guarantee does the tortoise come with? Can you have your vet examine the tortoise prior to purchase? How is the tortoise kept? How knowledgeable is the staff? The more questions you ask, the easier it will be to make your decision, and the more you know about Redfoot tortoises, the easier it will be to know what questions to ask.

Captive bred Redfoot tortoises can often be purchased from other tortoise enthusiasts. Check the advertisements in publications such as 'Reptiles Magazine'. Reptile swap meets can also be good places to find Redfoot tortoises, and many questions should be asked there as well. There are a number of large-scale tortoise breeders in the southern United States that work with Redfoot tortoises.

Health Examination
Before purchasing any tortoise, an overall examination should be made. See "Doing a Health Check" in the Health Issues section for a list of items you'll want to check over. Even if you're satisfied about the overall health of the tortoise, you may want to have your veterinarian examine it as well.

Other Considerations
You should ask yourself several questions before finally deciding to become a Redfoot owner. Do I have adequate space to house this tortoise, now and when it gets larger? Do I have time to take care of it properly? Am I prepared to care for this animal for many years? Now is the time to be honest with yourself, before you become attached to the tortoise - and you *will* become attached!

Enclosures – Considerations

Outside Pens
Redfoot tortoises get to be fairly large tortoises, and their pen needs to be big enough to allow them room to move around and have some space apart from other turtles. Larger pens also make it easier to provide a good temperature gradient, and provide enough room for water pans and hide houses. If you live in Florida or some other warm, sub-tropical area, you can keep them in an outside pen year round. People living in more temperate climates may have an outside pen in the summer, and an inside enclosure for the winter months. I live in central Illinois, and keep my Redfoot tortoises outdoors from May to September, and in a basement pen the rest of the year. If you live in a dry, arid place like Arizona, Redfoot tortoises may have a hard time of it outdoors, since they require a humid environment. You may need to spray down the enclosure several times a day to keep the humidity level up in dry climates.

Predators must be considered when planning an outdoor enclosure. Raccoons, opossums, hawks and owls can prey on small turtles, and even dogs can be a problem. A pen covered with chicken wire, hardware cloth, or framed wooden lattice may be necessary. You can't be with your turtles all of the time and a pen secure from predators and escapes will bring you peace of mind and make the experience more enjoyable. Avoid tempting dishonest people by placing pens where they cannot be seen from the sidewalk or street.

Talk to your neighbors about your plans. Having an understanding with your neighbors about your tortoises is a good idea - finding your Redfoot munching its way through their garden is not a great way for your neighbors to discover your hobby! Informed neighbors will keep your tortoises in mind and let you know before using potentially harmful pesticides, and you may find them just as interested in your pets as you are!

Hatchling and juvenile Redfoot tortoises are probably best left indoors until they acquire some size - you can bring them outside for some sun and exercise. Remember - small turtles have very little mass and can overheat rapidly and fatally in direct sun! Make sure they have a shady area to retreat to and cool off.

Inside Enclosures

Living in a small apartment, or in a temperate zone far from the tropics, should not keep you from becoming a Redfoot keeper. Hatchlings and juveniles can be well maintained in a modest enclosure for a number of years before you need to think about something bigger. Larger inside enclosures can be set up in basements, laundry rooms, and so on. I know of one keeper who converted her apartment balcony into a warm weather tortoise run! Keeping tortoises indoors means that you'll need to work a little harder to get your Redfoot enough natural sunlight, and methods for doing so are covered elsewhere in this book.

Outdoor Pens – Components and Materials

Shade
An outdoor pen is ideal for larger Redfoot tortoises. They can get exercise and plenty of sunlight, and are more likely to reproduce if kept outdoors. Temperature ranges must be taken into consideration when planning a pen. Plenty of shade needs to be provided for very hot days; shade helps Redfoot tortoises feel more secure as well. Trees and shrubs can be used to provide shade, and wooden lattice can be used to break up sunlight.

Hide House
A hide house is simply a covered, box-like structure made of wood or some other material, large enough to hold all of your tortoises. Redfoot tortoises will use the hide house for sleeping at night, and to cool off in the shade during hot afternoons. The hide house also functions as a sanctuary – a stress-free place away from the rest of the world. Plastic dog houses work very well as hide houses, and several can be used to hold multiple tortoises. Large hide houses can be constructed out of

plywood, and adding a second entrance cuts down on "traffic jams". The hide house should be placed in permanent shade, to avoid overheating the interior. A ceramic heat bulb can be used to warm the hide house on cool nights, but keep in mind, the hide house needs to be vented to prevent heat from reaching extreme temperatures.

Water Pans

Many different containers can be used as water pans, but all must meet several requirements; it must be shallow, easily accessible, and easy to clean. Redfoot tortoises are heavy tortoises and will not float, and will drown in water over their heads. Aluminum cake pans and casserole dishes work well; I use shallow stainless steel pans used in cafeteria steam tables. Plastic dish pans can be cut down a few inches, and the lids to plastic garbage cans make good water pans that are large enough to soak in. Small bodies of water heat quickly in the sun, so water pans should always be placed in the shade. Use several water pans for groups of tortoises.

Pen Materials

An enclosure of solid material is preferable. If provided with a ground level view out of the pen, tortoises may spend much of their time trying to crawl out! The walls should be high enough to keep the tortoises from climbing out - keep in mind that they can crawl on top of other tortoises! I build my pens to a minimum of twenty inches (.5m) in height. My Redfoot's outdoor pen is built partially under our sundeck, out of concrete block. The wall, including the cap block, is twenty inches (.5m) high. The pen extends east of the deck to provide a sunny, open area. The pen roughly measures 8 feet by 16 feet (2.4m by 4.87 m). It is an adequate space for several pairs of adult Redfoot tortoises.

Many tortoise species are burrowers by nature, and may dig underneath the walls of an enclosure. Fortunately, Redfoot tortoises are not accomplished excavators, and so extending the pen walls more than a few inches below ground level is not necessary.

There are plenty of materials available to construct a pen. Large galvanized stock tanks can be used to quickly set up a pen and are available from farm supply stores. Cement block is a popular favorite, allowing pens of irregular shapes. A cement block wall two blocks high is sufficient, and topping it off with solid "cap blocks" gives the enclosure a finished look, and a place to sit with your tortoises! Landscape timbers can also be used to construct a "turtle corral" in short time. Plywood can be used to construct a simple box pen, but is not very pleasing to the eye and can be damaged in a windstorm.

Chain link fence has limitations; tortoises of all kinds can bull their way right under a chain link fence, making tie-downs or landscape timbers along fence lines necessary. Bartlett (1999) uses lengths of 36 inch (91 cm) wide aluminum sheeting joined at the ends into a ring, with one edge sunk 12 inches (30 cm) into the ground.

Plants in the Pen

Redfoot tortoises will attempt to dine on any plant material inside their enclosure, so this must be taken into consideration. There are many common plants that can be poisonous to tortoises, including many popular landscaping plants, such as yew. Any harmless plants may be eaten past the point of recovery in a smaller pen, so it may be best to avoid most small plants aside from grasses and dandelions. Using pots or planters can help to keep tortoises away from plants. The enclosure can be built around bushes and trees to take advantage of their shade and provide added beauty.

Substrates

You can retain a patch of lawn grass, but you may find it eaten and worn away before long in a smaller pen. A hardwood mulch such as cypress makes a good substrate, cypress being a rot-resistant, inert wood. Avoid overly aromatic and resinous pine, cedar or eucalyptus mulches, as the fumes can be irritating and harmful. A mix of fine peat moss and sand also works well. Turtle poop can be handled and disposed of as you would for a dog. If you are planning to breed your Redfoot tortoises, the character of the soil becomes an important factor. Tightly packed clay soil makes it difficult for the female to dig her nest, and if unable to do so, she may retain the eggs and eventually deposit them on the surface or in a water pan. Turn the soil over to a depth of nearly a foot to loosen it and make it easier for the female to dig. Highfield (1996) recommends creating a nesting area with a gentle slope, preferably facing south.

Indoor Enclosures

Aquariums

For juvenile Redfoot tortoises, aquariums are one simple answer to housing. Long, shallow tanks make it easier to provide a temperature gradient, and provide easier access. Forty gallon "breeder" tanks work great - they are fairly long, and wider than conventional aquariums, and shallow as well. Any shop specializing in tropical fish can order one if they don't carry them in stock. Tortoises are confused by glass and will try to crawl through it, however - an opaque border can be placed around the perimeter of the tank to prevent this. Wallpaper border can be used to provide a decorative touch. Drawbacks: aquariums can be difficult to heat from above. Small aquariums should be avoided, as a proper temperature gradient cannot be established (see the Heat section), and may overheat. Another disadvantage large aquariums have is that their bulk and weight can make them hard to clean properly.

Sweater Boxes

There are many types of containers now available that are made of durable, opaque or transparent plastic. There are a number of sizes and shapes that a perfect for housing small sized Redfoot tortoises. Lightweight, inexpensive plastic containers are easy to clean and easy to move around. Heat lamps and full spectrum light fixtures can be fastened on one end or positioned overhead. A border (kitchen shelf contact paper works well) can be added around the outside.

Tortoise Tables
Are you handy with tools? You might consider building a tortoise table, which is simply a large wooden tray with sturdy legs. The sides are just tall enough to contain small to medium sized tortoises. The wooden surfaces can be sealed with waterproof marine paint, or stained and sealed with a non-toxic varnish such as Varathane Diamond®. Some people have built tables with multiple trays, which look much like a bunk bed of sorts, and have cutouts for water pans in order to sink them flush with the table surface!

Indoor Pens
Tortoise owners have shown no end of creativity in constructing indoor pens. A pen may be as simple as a plywood box knocked together, or as elaborate as a custom-designed cabinet. One person's ingenious solution to a simple pen was to purchase and assemble an inexpensive "woodgrain" bookcase, laying it down on its back and leaving out the shelves! In past years I built a cement block pen in my basement, with eight inches of topsoil and mulch on top of a plastic liner. Oval galvanized stock tanks are sometimes narrow enough to fit through wide doors. Black plastic tubs used for mixing mortar work well for smaller turtles, as do small plastic "kiddie pools". Some people use a spare room or a laundry room to house their Redfoot tortoises, and a few brave souls give them the run of the house, although this is not recommended due to the risk of damage and injury.

Furnishings for Indoor Enclosures
As with outdoor pens, a hide house should be installed on the cooler end of the enclosure. A plastic dishpan turned over and with a large entrance cut in one end, makes a great hide house for smaller tortoises. Broken clay flower pots, or butter and margarine tubs with doors cut in them can still be of service as a hide for juvenile or hatchling tortoises.

Square aluminum cake/brownie pans fit well in a corner as a water dish; jar lids and plastic plant saucers can be used for hatchlings. Remember to make sure there is easy access to and from the water pan, and keep an inch or less of water in it, as hatchlings and juveniles can easily drown. As a good rule of thumb with small tortoises is to have the water level no higher than the turtle's head when pulled into the shell.

For substrate, newspaper is hard to beat for use with smaller tortoises (big ones will pull it apart by simply crawling around). It is cheap, absorbent, and easy to replace. A hardwood mulch such as cypress can be used, but pine and other resinous mulches should be avoided. Hatchlings of other species are often kept on a layer of rabbit or guinea pig pellets, an absorbent material that can also be safely consumed. The humidity requirements of Redfoot tortoises may prohibit this, however.

Bathing and Exercise

Bathing
Your tortoise will welcome a soak in a pan or tub of water once or twice a week; it keeps the shell clean, and the skin on the legs, tail, and head supple. A tub or pan just a bit larger than the tortoise will do nicely and are easier to manage than large tubs. In the winter I use a plastic slop sink, which has a drain tied into the plumbing. The water should not be too cold or too warm - try to keep it near the temperature of the enclosure to avoid chilling or overheating your tortoise. You can clean up really dirty tortoises with a wash cloth or a soft brush and a bit of liquid hand soap, being careful to avoid the eyes.

Small Redfoot tortoises can have a nice soak in any small container that they cannot climb out of. Use a small amount of water to avoid drowning accidents - just enough to reach the head at rest.
Don't be surprised if your Redfoot defecates while soaking. This is a normal behavior for most tortoises. Give them a chance to finish before cleaning up the pan or tub and continuing the bath. Ten to fifteen minutes should be enough - you don't want your tortoise sitting in water that has grown cold!

Exercise
This is probably the most underrated aspect of tortoise health and well being. Your Redfoot needs regular activity to maintain good muscle tone, to promote proper growth and development, and to keep the appetite stimulated. In a large outdoor pen, this may not be much of an issue, but with smaller enclosures, and smaller Redfoot tortoises, you will have to be in charge of your tortoise's physical fitness program. After some time, your tortoise will have explored every corner of its enclosure, and its activity level may drop off somewhat. It's time to plunk your Redfoot down somewhere else for some exercise. A new environment helps to stimulate activity, whether it's a walk in the park or a crawl around the living room. With smaller tortoises, a supervised swim in a few inches of water is a great way to provide a good workout. Exercise - one more thing to keep in the back of your mind!

Nutrition

The importance of good nutrition cannot be underestimated. Tortoise nutrition is much like our own as far as separating facts from fiction, and the discussion can get as complex as we let it. I have tried to keep the subject as simple as possible, and to key in on the really important factors, and yet nutrition is the largest part of this care sheet, and broken into two sections. Here's how I break it down:

- Water
- Variety
- Calcium and Phosphorus
- The Good Stuff!

- Problem Foods
- Supplements
- Protein
- Prepared Foods
- How Much? How Often?
- Feeding Redfoot tortoises - One Keeper's Approach
- Consequences of a Poor Diet

Fortunately, you can build a good diet for your Redfoot tortoises right from the supermarket. Now members of your family, your tortoise's needs are just a few more lines on the grocery list each week. Most of the good foods they need are readily available and inexpensive, such as greens. Once you get into a routine, the amount of time you spend 'foraging' for your Redfoot tortoises can be reduced to a reasonable amount of time.

Water
There is no element of nutrition more important than water. It is essential to all processes in the body, from the cellular level upwards. Provide your Redfoot tortoises with fresh water every day, in a shallow pan or dish with easy access. The water should never be more than several inches deep, because Redfoot tortoises are heavy tortoises regardless of size, and can easily sink and drown! There are some unresolved concerns about chlorine ingestion in reptiles, so play it safe and use a tropical fish de-chlorinator to treat drinking water. Clean the water container often with soap and hot water. Redfoot tortoises will often climb in for a soak, if the container is large enough. If you are keeping your Redfoot outside, use a small container to prevent your tortoise from soaking in chilly water on cool days and nights.

Variety
Being primarily forest-edge and savanna dwellers, Redfoot tortoises eat fallen figs, plums, and other fruit. They consume the flowers and leaves of plants, fungi, insects and other invertebrates, and carrion. They are, in short, omnivores that consume a wide variety of food items. Your Redfoot needs the same wide selection of foods to ensure proper nutrition. The wider a variety of good foods provided the better chance you have of meeting your Redfoot tortoises' nutritional needs. There is no single food item that is nutritionally complete, so a 'narrow' diet is harmful over time. Redfoot tortoises can be finicky eaters if offered the same food all the time - they like variety! You may enjoy a good steak, but you probably would not like to eat one at every meal - keep that in mind when you feed your tortoise. Variety is the spice of life, and the key to good nutrition.

Calcium and Phosphorus
In order to put together a proper diet for your tortoises, it is necessary to understand the relationship between calcium and phosphorus and how they affect chelonian metabolism, growth, and health. The calcium-to-phosphorus ratio is discussed here and in the 'Lighting' section later. Calcium and phosphorus are both important elements necessary for building and strengthening teeth and bone. They are vital to proper neuromuscular function, cell health and cell replication. A deficiency of either element can cause severe health problems.

A balance must be maintained between calcium and phosphorus. Excess phosphorus inhibits the absorption and utilization of calcium, which can lead to Metabolic Bone Disease (MBD), and poor health in general (MBD is discussed in more detail in the Consequences of a Poor Diet Section). A ratio between these two elements has emerged from research into reptile nutrition - the rule of thumb for proper intake of these elements a minimum of two parts calcium to one part phosphorus. This means your Redfoot tortoises' diet should have this minimum 2:1 Calcium - to - Phosphorus ratio as an end result. For example, if I feed one cup of papaya with a 4.5:1 Ca/P ratio, I can add a cup of zucchini with a 1:2 Ca/P ratio, and come close to my desired 2:1 mark overall. Adding a phosphorus-free calcium supplement once or twice a week will help ensure a proper calcium intake. It is important to realize that Phosphorus is plentiful in fruits and green vegetation, whereas calcium is commonly deficient.

The 2:1 Ca/P ratio is important, but not to the point that foods with a 'bad' ratio should be excluded. Many fruits and vegetables have a poor Ca/P ratio, but are still nutritionally valuable. If you design your Redfoot' tortoises' diet around a base of fruits and vegetables with a 'good' Ca/P ratio, then you can feed them a wide variety of foods. In addition to keeping your turtles happy with a wide selection of foods, it will ensure that you meet all of the nutritional requirements across the board - vitamins and minerals, proteins, carbohydrates, and fats.

A final bit of advice on the Ca/P ratio; keep it in mind, but don't obsess over it! It is important to know, however, that the younger the tortoise, and the more rapid its rate of growth, the more critical this aspect of diet is. Juveniles can develop calcium deficiencies very quickly compared to an adult.

The Good Stuff
Here's a short list of fruits and vegetables with a good Ca/P ratio (shown rounded to the nearest whole number):

- collard, mustard greens, 8:1
- papaya, 5:1
- parsley, 3:1
- dandelion greens, 3:1
- kale, 3:1
- figs, 2:1
- prickly pear pads, 2:1

What else will your Redfoot like to eat? How about strawberries, blueberries, mango, citrus, or melon? You can offer string beans, okra, cucumbers, zucchini, tomatoes, turnip greens. It is a picky tortoise indeed that would refuse any of these foods. In general, leafy vegetables and flowers should form the base of what's offered each day, with some fruit mixed in. Try to mix and match the foods you offer - make each day a surprise!

Problem Foods
There are certain groups of foods that cause nutritional havoc and should be avoided or offered only in small amounts. The first of these groups are those plants

containing oxalic acid, which binds with calcium and prevents it from being metabolized, forming calcium oxalate, a salt that accumulates in the kidneys. Spinach has a lovely Ca/P ratio, but unfortunately it is one of these "oxalates". Others include rhubarb, beets and their greens, swiss chard, and celery. It is probably best to avoid them altogether.

Another group worth mentioning is the "brassicas", which include cabbage, kale, cauliflower, broccoli, bok choi, brussels sprouts, turnips, and rutabagas. In quantity, they can interfere with the activity of the thyroid gland, and can lead to goiter, a swelling of the thyroid. There's no problem in offering these as one element of a varied menu, but they should not be used as a mainstay of the diet.

There isn't a tortoise on this planet that would turn its nose up at sweet, juicy, iceberg lettuce. Unfortunately, iceberg lettuce is a nutritionally bankrupt food item. Iceberg, looseleaf, romaine, and other lettuces have low percentages of vitamins and minerals and (excepting looseleaf) have terrible Ca/P ratios. If you offer lettuces regularly, you may find your Redfoot tortoises ignoring other foods while scarfing down every last bit of lettuce! Feed them sparingly or not at all.
Redfoot tortoises and many other tortoises love bananas. Unfortunately, like the sweet lettuces, banana has a backwards Ca/P ratio, and tortoises can become addicted and refuse other foods. Offer banana sparingly. One good use for banana is to hide calcium and vitamin supplements, since many tortoises will turn their noses up at food with supplements sprinkled on top. The powder can be mixed in with mashed banana and will be overlooked by banana-loving Redfoot tortoises!

Canned dog and cat food should be kept out of the diet; both contain too much fat, too much protein, and you run the risk of your tortoises ignoring other foods in favor of this one.

Supplements
Adding a calcium and Vitamin D3 supplement (one without phosphorus) on a regular basis helps to meet the needed requirements. You should not rely on the supplement to provide all of the needed calcium - that's why they're called supplements! A varied diet with foods rich in calcium will meet most of your tortoises' needs. Many keepers add a cuttle bone or two to their turtle pens. Sold for pet birds, cuttle bones supply calcium and help to keep bird beaks in proper trim - and they work the same way for turtles! Some Redfoot tortoises will turn their noses up at food with powdered supplements sprinkled on it. You can fool a finicky Redfoot by mixing supplements in with some mashed aromatic fruit like strawberries, banana, or papaya. Keep in mind that you can easily 'oversupplement' your tortoise, and tax its liver and kidneys in the process. Multivitamin supplements are completely unnecessary if your tortoises are eating a varied, healthy diet, as previously described. Remember: Sunlight is necessary to metabolize calcium. Diet, sunlight, water, exercise and a proper environment all work together to keep your Redfoot in top condition!

Protein
Proteins are used to build skin, shell, muscle and connective tissues, indeed, the very cells themselves. Proteins are broken down into amino acids by the digestive process, and the body then reassembles the amino acids into useful proteins. Proteins can also be metabolized or "burned off" like carbohydrates, or converted by the liver into stored fat. Animal proteins contain a wide array of essential amino acids, and are referred to as complete proteins; plant-derived proteins contain a somewhat narrower subset of amino acids, and so are called incomplete proteins. Your Redfoot needs both types of protein in its diet. Good sources of protein for Redfoot tortoises include:

- Dry dog food (brands that contain both animal and plant derived proteins)
- Commercially prepared turtle/tortoise foods
- Pinkie mice, or frozen-then-thawed small adult mice
- String beans, lima beans

It's good to remember that most plants have at least small quantities of incomplete proteins.

Protein deficiencies affect growth and can cause deformities and abnormal growth. The immune system is weakened, and energy levels and muscle response are affected as well. Too much protein affects liver and kidney function, and can pyramiding of the shell. In recent years, tortoise keepers have realized that protein intake should be much smaller than what was previously accepted. Proteins should be a minor element of your Redfoot tortoises' diet, even for young, growing juveniles. Offer it once or twice a week at the most, in small amounts.

Prepared Foods
In recent years a number of commercially prepared foods for reptiles have been developed and people have many opinions as to their efficacy and use. Many experienced tortoise keepers feel that most prepared tortoise diets to contain far too much protein than most adult tortoises need, an opinion I share.

On the other side of the coin, prepared diets from Walkabout Farms are a promising source of supplemental nutrition. Their 'Forest Tortoise' diet is designed to be used as a supplement given with a greens-and-fruit salad. I have not used their products at this time, and so cannot offer an opinion on them. A number of Redfoot keepers are using the Forest Tortoise diet without complaint. Pay a visit to Walkabout's website at **www.herpnutrition.com** for more details.

Prepared foods, if used at all, should be one element of the overall diet, and never a mainstay, even for growing young Redfoot tortoises. I currently use a floating food stick designed for aquatic turtles, such as Wardley's Reptile Ten or Tetra's Reptomin, because they contain both animal and plant proteins. I also occasionally substitute 'Iams' brand dry dog food. I offer a quarter cup once a week to my adult Redfoot tortoises, sprinkled atop their regular food.

How much? How often?
How much you feed depends on a number of factors. An adult male Redfoot has different requirements than a breeding female, or a growing juvenile. As an

example, Joey, my adult male, consumes between 1 and 1.5 cups of food at a feeding, whereas Iris, an adult, breeding female, can easily consume twice that amount. I feed them two days in a row, and then skip two days.

To figure out the proper amounts, measure how much food is offered, and how much (if any) is left uneaten. Observe your tortoise during feeding. Is all of the food consumed at a single sitting? If you have more than one Redfoot, does one eat more or less that another? It is not always necessary to feed the same amount of food at each feeding, either. Bear in mind, captive tortoises with caring owners eat much better than wild tortoises! Most tortoise keepers are of the opinion that slow, steady growth is the best plan for the health and well being of their Redfoot tortoises. It is a difficult approach for many people, because they feel they are underfeeding their tortoises, and thus not caring for them properly. Too much food, and too much protein can cause unnaturally fast growth, which can result in a misshapen, pyramided shell.

You may want to feed your Redfoot every day, but it is not necessary to do so. Smaller amounts should be offered during daily feedings, and you may find that your Redfoot may not eat every day. Adult Redfoot tortoises can be fed every other day, or even every third day. Missing food for a few days will not cause harm, but your tortoises certainly will be hungry! Try to establish a routine that works for you and stick with it. As a general rule, foods such as Hibiscus flowers or pieces of de-spined Opuntia cactus may be offered fairly freely without any risk whatever.

Feeding Redfoot tortoises - One Keeper's Approach
Typically, I make a salad with several basic components - greens, fruit, and a non-leafy vegetable. The greens are always collard, mustard, turnip, or kale. These greens all have a great calcium/phosphorus ratio, so they make a good base that I can mix in other foods that they like, but may not be so nutritious. I add fruit, but usually not in large quantities. I make enough salad for two days, and I usually feed two days in a row, and then skip two days. All food items are carefully washed to remove pesticides and waxes.

For fruit, I use papaya most of all - Redfoot tortoises love it, and it has an excellent Ca/P ratio. I also rotate in banana, mango, and any other non-citrus fruit on hand. When we buy blueberries and strawberries and such, the tortoises get their share too. Banana is a wonderful agent for hiding calcium supplements by simply mashing it all together, but should not be a regularly offered fruit.

Other vegetables - prickly pear cactus pads (Opuntia) are another nutritious food that my Redfoot tortoises love. I offer it several times a week when it is available. I also rotate in zucchini, okra, summer squash, and string beans, all in small quantities. I try to avoid the more obvious oxalates (calcium binders) like cabbage, broccoli, and so on, but they may get a small amount once in a great while.

Everything is chopped fairly fine and mixed well, so when they go for their favorites, they have to take in the necessaries as well. I think the fruit juices or banana paste makes it all taste good. Once a week they get a small amount of dog food or Wardley Reptile Ten Sticks for protein, and once a week on another day I add a calcium/D3 supplement. Sometimes a meal is just a small snack - I'll throw in an ear of sweet corn once in a great while, or perhaps some chopped pears or chunks of pumpkin or squash. If there's leftover salad from dinner, they get that - romaine and red leaf lettuce typically, maybe with some carrot, mushrooms and tomato. It's hard to find an herbivore that doesn't like romaine, but I don't think it's a good staple compared to greens.

Consequences of a poor or mismanaged diet

- Metabolic Bone Disease (MBD): A calcium deficiency, resulting in softened bones (including the shell) and weakened muscles. Prolonged MBD in growing turtles results in deformities, stunted growth, and death. Varied causes include a lack of calcium, too much phosphorus, a lack of Vitamin D3, a lack of sunlight, or any combination of the above.

- Kidney failure: Often caused by excess protein over a prolonged period of time. Kidney function can also be impaired by dehydration and maintenance at inadequate levels of humidity.

- Pyramiding or tenting of the carapace: Results from excess protein in the diet and inadequate calcium or Vitamin D3. It is not clear whether the pyramiding itself poses a health risk, but in Redfoot tortoises it is a sure indicator of excess protein, which has other more dire consequences.

- Reproduction problems: An improper diet can affect many aspects of reproduction - ovulation may not occur, fewer eggs may be produced, there may not be enough resources to produce healthy offspring, reproduction itself may not take place.

Metabolic Bone Disease In Detail
The calcium and phosphorus used to create bone comes from the bloodstream, where concentrations of both elements are maintained in the blood plasma. When a deficiency of either mineral occurs and the plasma concentrations become low enough, bone mineralization ceases. The mineralization (or more precisely, calcification) process gives rigidity and strength to bone tissue. If other elements of the diet are normal, bone tissue may continue to be produced, but is never mineralized. As a result, the animal may continue to grow, but the bones are weak, easily broken, and easily deformed during the growth process. During a prolonged calcium deficiency, calcium may be resorbed from bone back into the bloodstream, accelerating MBD. If caught in time, MBD can be stopped and the animal saved from death, but physical affects of the condition may be irreversible if too much time has passed.

Shell Pyramiding In Detail
Too much protein also can have dire consequences. The liver and kidneys are taxed, and complete kidney failure can occur. With Redfoot tortoises and other species of tortoises, excess protein can result in the overproduction of outer shell material, or keratin, on the carapace. When keratin production outstrips growth, it gets deposited in thicker than normal layers from underneath the scute. The

thickening scute soon takes on a "domed" or "tented" appearance. The raised scutes are in stark contrast to the scutes of a Redfoot with a normal protein intake, and a clear indicator of past dietary imbalances.

Redfoot tortoises should have a carapace with smooth, slightly curved scutes. Excess protein problems can be avoided simply by keeping protein intake as one regular element of the diet - it should never be a staple of the diet. Remember that adult tortoises need less protein than growing ones do, and growing ones need less than you think. With a young, growing Redfoot, the tenting appearance can smooth out somewhat over time, once protein levels are reduced, but may never totally disappear.

Light

As with all other reptiles, the light and heat of the sun is used by tortoises to regulate internal body temperatures, but the issue of light is more complicated than thermoregulation:

- Vitamin D3 is necessary for reptiles to metabolize the calcium in their diet.
- Most reptiles cannot store Vitamin D3 in their bodies.
- Reptiles use a part of the ultraviolet wavelengths in sunlight to synthesize Vitamin D3.

Lack of sunlight results in a calcium uptake deficiency. Bones and shells soften, and in young turtles and other reptiles, bones do not grow to proper size and shape, resulting in deformities, stunted growth, and often a short life. Calcium supplements without sunlight are ineffective, and Vitamin D3 supplements are not a complete substitute. Redfoot tortoises kept in outdoor pens receive sufficient sunlight, even in well-shaded pens. Getting sufficient sunlight to tortoises kept indoors is a challenge, and there are a number of solutions to the problem.

Outdoor Excursions For Indoor Turtles
In temperate climates, your Redfoot tortoises can be taken outside for a bit of sun during the warmer months. A few hours of sun a week goes a long way to meet the needs of your tortoise. I know a woman who packs up her tortoises in a laundry basket and takes them to the park! There are several things to remember when taking your Redfoot tortoises out for a walk:

- Turtles can rapidly overheat in direct sun, especially small ones with little mass. Use shaded or partially shaded areas - there are still plenty of photons whizzing around!
- Turtles are faster than you think, and can cover vast distances when your back is turned. Never leave your pets unattended.

Temporary pens can be set up for basking purposes. Wire dog crates and rabbit pens work well for smaller tortoises, and secondhand infant 'playpens' have been used by some people. Sun decks and balconies can also be used for sunning.

Top to bottom, from left:

1. Beautiful male 'Cherry Head' Redfoot.
2. Mating pair.
3. Male circles female bobbing his head and biting at her front legs.
4. Plastron of a male Redfoot. Note depressed plastron, long tail, and marked 'waist' that is diagnostic of sex in this species.

Photos on this page by A. C. Highfield.

A. C. Highfield

Mike Pingleton

Mike Pingleton

Top to bottom, from left:

1. A suitable feed mix comprising green leaves and flowers. Soft fruits should also be provided.
2. Evidence of scute 'pyramiding' - a consequence of excess protein and lack of dietary calcium.
3. A small container with suitable substrate for a small juvenile.
4. A warm, well-insulated unit designed for overnight accommodation of Redfoot tortoises, as provided by an expert keeper in S. California.

A. C. Highfield

Examples of indoor and outdoor accommodation for Redfoot tortoises. High levels of ambient humidity and fresh water for soaking must always be available.

Photos on this page by Mike Pingleton

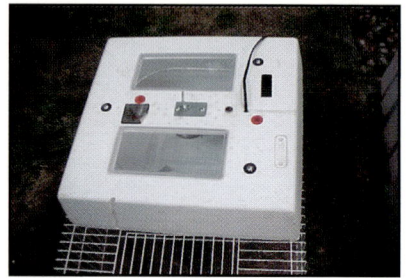

Top to bottom:

1. A female excavates her nest.
2. The eggs are deposited in the nest.
3. A 'Hovabator' incubator in use.
4. A hatchling emerges!
5. The remaining egg-sac will be absorbed over the first few days and the plaston and carapace will straighten out.
6. The egg tooth is clearly visble on this newly emerged hatchling.
7. Eggs rest in a tray containing moist Vermiculite. The thermometer probes are clearly visible in this shot.

Photos on this page by Mike Pingleton

"Walking" your Redfoot tortoises has other benefits. They receive some exercise, which helps maintain good muscle tone, and stimulates the appetite. They get to explore new environments and landscapes, which I believe is good for their well-being in less tangible ways - the interior of an enclosure can get mighty familiar in a short time!

The Light Through Yon Window
Putting your Redfoot near a sunny window seems like the simple answer to the sunlight problem. However, the glass in most windows reflects away the ultraviolet wavelengths needed for D3 synthesis. Of course, windows can be opened during warmer weather. During the winter, a window can be opened for brief periods on sunny days. In the mornings and afternoons, the light comes in at a lower angle and strikes further inside the window, allowing your turtle to bask well away from a cold draft. You can place your turtle on a dark fabric or other material, which will absorb heat and help keep your turtle warm while it basks. A heating pad also works well for this purpose, and you can always point a small space heater at your Redfoot. A half hour of sunlight a week during the winter (weather permitting) will go a long way to meet your turtle's needs.

Light Fixtures, Reptile Bulbs
Redfoot tortoises kept indoors will need lighting for D3 synthesis. There are a number of companies today producing "full spectrum" fluorescent tubes designed to meet the requirements of reptiles. Each brand of bulb produces varying amounts of light in the ultraviolet wavelength, but the issue is complicated. The ultraviolet (UV) wavelength is divided into two parts, UVA and UVB. Plants use the UVA part of the spectrum, while reptiles use the UVB section for D3 synthesis. A "plant bulb" emits UVA, but little or none of the needed UVB spectrum, and so are of little use. When selecting a bulb, check the package for a spectral analysis chart, to make sure the bulb emits UVB. **Note:** "Black light" bulbs that emit solely UVB rays (often referred to as "black light blue" or "UV blue" bulbs) can be dangerous to animals and humans, and should be avoided. The new 'UVB-Heat' lamps manage to combine genuinely high levels of UV-B output with heat (unlike fluorescent tubes), and many keepers have reported excellent results with these.

To be effective, fluorescent reptile tubes need to be placed between twelve and eighteen inches above your turtles. After time, the bulbs become ineffective as the emitted wavelength narrows; replace them every six months or so. Mercury vapor 'UVB-Heat' lamps last longer, and a yearly replacement should suffice.

Photoperiods
Being tropical tortoises, Redfoot tortoises live where the days are long. Give yours twelve to fourteen hours of light each day. Use a lamp timer to keep a regular photoperiod. One more thing to remember - Redfoot tortoises sleep at night, so a ten to twelve hour 'dark' period is important, too!

NATURAL DIETS OF TROPICAL FOREST TORTOISES (*GEOCHELONE CARBONARIA* and *G. DENTICULATA*)

	Red-Foot and Yellow-foot tortoise diet in Brazil *(after Moskovits and Bjorndal, 1990, Pritchard and Trebbau, 1984)*
Forage plants consumed, leaves, stalks, flowers:	Unidentified grasses, palm frond, vine stems, unidentified green leaves.
Flowers only or stem and flowers only consumed:	*Jacaranda copaia, Cochlospermum orinocense, Mauritia flexuosa*
Fruits consumed:	*Spondias lutea, Anacardium gigantea, Philodendron sp., Bromiliad sp., Passiflora coccinea, P. verspertillo, Mauritia flexuosa, Duguetia surinamensis, Genipa americana, Pradosia sp., Clavija sp., Ficus sp., Annona Sp.*
Seeds consumed:	Unknown.
Carrion consumed:	Agouti, peccary, bird, snake, lizard, and deer carcasses.
Live prey consumed:	Snails, ants, termites, bees, beetles, butterflies.
Miscellaneous items:	Mushrooms (several species), sand, soil, pebbles, tortoise feces, bark.

From: 'The Tortoise & Turtle Feeding Manual' by A. C. Highfield (Carapace Press, 2000)

Heat

As with all reptiles, Redfoot tortoises should be provided with a temperature gradient in their enclosure - it should be warmer on one end, cooler on the other, within the acceptable range limits. This allows the tortoises to thermoregulate, that is, adjust their body temperature by moving to different parts of the enclosure. Typically, a heat source (basking lamp) is placed on one end of the enclosure, and a hide box on the other end or in the middle. The bigger the enclosure, the easier it is to provide a gradient. In homes with air conditioning, it may be necessary to use a heating pad or other device to maintain a safe temperature at night when the basking light is off.

Maintaining proper temperatures for your Redfoot tortoises is a big part of keeping them healthy. With reptiles, heat is an important factor in proper digestion, and maintaining a healthy appetite.. As with humans, the immune system depends on warm, stable body temperatures; when the temperature remains too cool for a period of time, the immune system shuts down, and infection and disease can take their toll.

Heat sources are an important element in providing a temperature gradient for your tortoises, and there are a number of ways to do so. There are several things to remember when choosing a heat source:

- The entire enclosure should not be heated - heat one end or one part.
- The animal should be able to easily move away from a heat source.
- It is preferable to provide heat from above when possible.
- Heat sources should be controlled with either a thermostat or a timer, and temperature ranges should be tested and established before the tortoise is introduced to the enclosure.
- Strive to establish a daytime high at least in the middle 80s °F (28-30 °C) and a nighttime temperature no lower that 70° (21 °C).
- Hiding places should be placed away from heat sources and cool areas. Never make a shy animal choose security over an uncomfortable temperature!

The best investment you can make is a good indoor/outdoor electronic thermometer. Get one that retains high and low temperatures in memory; you can use this feature to test high and low temperatures over a twenty four hour period. Temperatures can climb over a period of time and this method is more accurate than simply spot-checking temperatures with a regular thermometer. Be safe, be sure, get a good thermometer. See Radio Shack and other similar stores; indoor-outdoor thermometers are usually under twenty dollars. Some even feature a hygrometer to measure humidity, useful with Redfoot tortoises and other tortoises.

Heat Sources

Basking Lamps
Available in most hardware stores, a clip-on lamp with an aluminum reflector makes a versatile basking lamp. It can be clamped on one end of an enclosure or suspended overhead, and can be plugged into a timer to shut off the light at night. The heat produced depends on the light bulb wattage, so start with a low wattage bulb and check the surface temperature with an electronic thermometer.

Ceramic Heat Bulbs
One of the best ways to heat an enclosure is to use a ceramic heat bulb in a reflector lamp. These bulbs produce heat by emitting infrared light, which is radiated through a ceramic housing. These bulbs heat evenly and their warmth penetrates deeper into your tortoise, and since they produce no visible light, they can be used at night. My Redfoot tortoises prefer them over light bulbs. When properly placed they are completely safe to use and last far longer than conventional bulbs. One thing to remember: ceramic bulbs should be used with a ceramic socket, since they get warm enough to melt a plastic socket. Ceramic fixtures are available at hardware stores and there are several reflector lamps available with ceramic sockets. Ceramic bulbs come in a variety of wattages, and the lower wattage bulbs work well for smaller enclosures. As with other heat sources, use an electronic thermometer to establish proper temperatures.

Heating Pads
Designed for human use, they are sturdy, and have 2-3 temperature settings. Heating pads can be useful in homes with cool temperatures, keeping the enclosure warm at night. The pad can be put on a separate timer to switch on when the basking light is switched off. Make sure not to rest an enclosure directly on the pad, since the weight can damage the heating element. Wooden strips can be used to elevate the enclosure, and the heating pad can be slid underneath. I have used heating pads safely in this manner for many years and prefer them as a supplemental heat source in cool conditions. Heating pads are also useful for sick tortoises with colds and respiratory infections.

Space Heaters - Baseboard and other types of electric space heaters can be used to heat a room or large enclosure. Make sure they are placed where they cannot be moved or tipped over, or where animals can come in contact with them. Kerosene and other fueled heaters should not be used indoors – the fumes resulting from combustion are deadly to tortoises and tortoise keepers alike!

Heat Tape / Pipe Wrap
Heat tape, of the type installed under ceramic tile in bathrooms, can be used in conjunction with a thermostat to regulate temperatures, provided you are experienced in electrical matters. Pipe wrap is designed to prevent exposed water pipes from freezing solid, and usually does not get warm enough to be of use. There are easier heating methods described here.

"Hot Rocks"
If you cut the cord off, they make a nice rock for your Redfoot to climb over; otherwise, don't use them. They get very hot, are uncontrollable, and tortoises don't thermoregulate by sitting on an extremely hot surface! Besides, having an animal defecate on a hot rock is a sure way to stink up your home!

Under-Tank Heaters
Probably should be avoided; most brands do not have temperature controls and get too hot. There are horror stories about malfunctioning under-tank heaters.

Things to remember:

- Avoid placing small enclosures in the path of heating/air conditioning ducts
- A covered aquarium will trap heat!
- In temperate climates, be prepared for seasonal temperature changes and monitor your enclosures carefully.
- Have a plan for power failures!

Health Issues

This section deals with symptoms of disease and other problems that can affect the health of your Redfoot. It does not prescribe any treatments; I recommend establishing a working relationship with a veterinarian experienced with reptilian health issues, and treating any maladies as the vet indicates.

Finding a veterinarian
Find a local veterinarian with experience in reptile medicine before you need one. If one cannot be located, perhaps your local veterinarian can consult with another experienced veterinarian.

A good way to find an experienced reptile vet is to visit the website of the Association of Reptilian and Amphibian Veterinarians (**www.arav.org**). Talk to your vet, tell him/her about your tortoises, find out if he/she has treated tortoises; in other words, get comfortable with your vet ahead of time! Take your tortoises in for an initial consultation.

Doing a health check
Check the overall appearance of your Redfoot tortoises each time you feed them. It's a good time to quickly scan them for problems, and you quickly learn what's normal as far as appearances and behavior are concerned. Talk with your veterinarian about any problems you might notice, and keep detailed notes. **Note**: these are also good guidelines for inspecting a tortoise you are considering purchasing.

Overall appearance: The tortoise should be active and alert. It should hold up its head, and follow movement. It should eat readily.

Eyes: The eyes should be clear and free of any crusty material. Both should readily track movement, and be completely open. Any redness or swelling could indicate conjunctivitis; swollen, half-opened eyes can indicate a Vitamin A deficiency or can indicate incorrect environmental maintenance (usually, too dry). Wet, teary eyes are common when there is insufficient humidity. Check the scales around the eyes for signs of mites.

Nose: The nasal passages should be dry and free of any crusty material. Any clear or yellow discharge, or bubbles forming in the nostril, can indicate an upper respiratory infection. Many tortoises can make a whistling or even a snorting sound on occasion when breathing, which can be normal - a regular, wet-sounding wheeze is not. A wet nose can also indicate insufficient humidity.

Mouth: The upper and lower beaks should be of proportionate size; overgrown and malformed beaks indicate a diet of foods too soft to provide normal wear. The beaks should be free of sores and discolorations, often seen with infectious stomatitis (mouth rot). Wheezing, gasping, or excess salivation may indicate an upper respiratory infection or pneumonia.

Ears: The outer ear covering should be flat and in profile with the lines of the neck. Any swelling about the ear or where the jaws meet can indicate an inner ear infection.

Skin: Check the neck and limbs for ticks and mites. Both can carry diseases; ticks should be carefully removed with tweezers and your vet can treat for mites. Check for cuts and sores, particularly on the feet, and the nails.

Shell: The shell should be hard and firm, without soft spots or soft edges. Shell softness can indicate Metabolic Bone Disease (MBD). Ulcerated or eroded areas can be indictors of shell rot, which is either bacterial or fungal in nature.

Stool: Redfoot poop normally can be either dry or somewhat runny, depending on what foods were eaten. Check the stool for undigested food, worms and worm segments, mucus, or blood. All are indicators of a parasitic infestation. The stool should be gathered and taken to the veterinarian along with the tortoise.

Urine: Like other tortoises from humid, water-rich environments, Redfoot tortoises normally excrete liquid urine, including urea and ammonia, and sometimes in large amounts. A dry, chalky urate deposit (which is normal in many arid land tortoises) should be looked into by a veterinarian. Redfoot tortoises will sometimes urinate copiously when under stress.

Parasites: Turtles of all kinds fall victim to a number of parasites, both externally and internally. They can inhabit the blood, the digestive tract, and other major organs. They range in size from single-celled organisms to ticks the size of your thumbnail. Some cause little harm to the host, while others can kill the animal. With many types of parasites, the turtle is weakened to the point where it cannot thrive, grow, or reproduce.

Some of the signs of parasitic infestation include:

- Weight loss
- Inactivity, listlessness
- Lack of appetite
- Little or no growth
- Unusual stool (undigested food, worms and worm segments, mucus, blood)
- Regurgitation of food items

Take a stool sample to the veterinarian along with the tortoise. The vet will examine the stool and may also draw a blood sample for examination. If parasites are found and a treatment is proscribed, all of the tortoises in your collection will need to be treated as well. Note: the drug known as Ivermectin is a very effective treatment for certain types of parasitic infections, but can be fatal when given to turtles - a good fact to keep in mind.

Redfoot tortoises kept outdoors can be prone to certain parasites. Even if your tortoises exhibit no symptoms of an infestation, it's a good idea to bring stool samples to your vet for analysis. Ask your vet how often checks should be made.

Any new tortoises, wild-caught ones in particular, should be quarantined and examined by a veterinarian before exposing the rest of your tortoises. Captive-bred hatchlings that are raised indoors generally carry little in the way of parasites, but should be observed for problems nonetheless.

Disease Prevention Practices

Quarantine: All new tortoises should be kept separate from others in your collection. Highfield (1996) recommends a six month quarantine at a minimum, preferably a year. Your veterinarian should examine any new quarantined animal. You should always wash your hands with soap and water before and after handling quarantined tortoises, and their eating and drinking utensils should not be interchanged with those of other animals.

Cleaning Habits: Food and water utensils should be thoroughly washed with soap and water, then sterilized with bleach or Betadine solution and rinsed well. Hands should be washed thoroughly with soap and water (or Betadine solution). The pen substrate should be changed regularly, and feces removed as often as possible. Soiled water bowls and food pans should be removed promptly and cleaned.

Mixing Species: Not recommended. Keep like species together. A tortoise from one geographical region may carry and have a resistance to a pathogen that another species may have no resistance to. See Highfield (1996) for more details on this subject.

Reproduction

Redfoot tortoises reach sexual maturity between eight and twelve years of age, with ten years being the approximate norm. They are usually 10-12 inches (25-30 cm) in length at this stage, with Cherry Heads being somewhat smaller at maturity.

Male or Female?

Male Redfoot tortoises typically have a concave plastron, which assists the male in mounting the female during copulation. The male's tail is longer and broader as well. Females have a flatter plastron (which may still be slightly concaved), and a narrower tail. Another difference shows in the notch between anal or posterior scutes on the plastron; in males, the notch is a wide angle, while the female has a narrower angle. Males can also have a "waist" or "peanut" shape when viewed from above, for reasons unknown. It can be very difficult to tell the sex of a hatchling or juvenile Redfoot tortoise. Comparisons can be made of multiple young turtles of the same size, but this is not a fool-proof method.

Courtship and Mating

Redfoot tortoises can breed throughout the year. Breeding is often triggered by rainy weather. Some courtship rituals have been observed on part of the males. The male often closely follows the female around for a time, and will smell the female's cloaca, possibly to confirm the sex (or perhaps the species) of the tortoise he is following. Sometimes the male will crawl ahead and tun around to face the female, and engage in a ritualistic movement of the head and neck. The neck is swayed side to side, and occasionally is bobbed up and down in a short arc. The male may grunt or "cluck" at this time, and may also exhale loudly through the nostrils. This behavior is also observed between two or more males competing for females. Multiple males also engage in butting and biting each other, and occasionally one gets turned over. Males of unequal size should be separated to avoid injury to the smaller tortoise.

Copulation is as typified among other turtles; the male climbs up on the female's carapace from behind, in order to bring the male's penis (normally enclosed in the tail) in contact with the female's cloaca, which the oviducts open into. The concavity in the male's plastron helps to hold him in place during copulation, which can last up to several hours. During copulation, the male Redfoot will oftentimes grunt or "cluck", while swaying head and neck from side to side. The "cluck" resembles that of a chicken, only much slower. The male can be quite loud – one of my neighbors got quite a surprise while searching for the 'chicken' loose in my back yard!

Egg Laying

Depending on diet, captive conditions and other factors, females may lay multiple clutches of eggs. Loman (1996) recounts captive females at his Florida facility laying eggs monthly for 3-4 months, skipping a month, then again laying monthly for 3-4 more months. My Redfoot tortoises, kept in a more temperate climate, produced clutches every five months. Clutch sizes between three and fifteen eggs have been reported in captivity and in the field.

When the female is ready to lay eggs, she will eat less or not at all. She will become more active, walking about the enclosure, sniffing the ground here and there. This activity may go on for several days. Once a spot with suitable temperature and humidity requirements is found, the female begins to dig the nest. She urinates on the spot to loosen the soil, and begins excavating a cavity with her rear legs. It may take her many hours to dig a hole deep enough; on the three occasions that I observed excavation, one hole was seven inches (18 cm) deep, another was nine inches (23 cm), and another was eleven inches (28 cm). During excavation, she may cluck or 'chuff' at any other tortoises that get too close.

After depositing the eggs, the female again uses her hind legs to fill in the hole, compacting the soil as she goes. When finished, it may be difficult to detect where the nest is - the female Redfoot does a good job of hiding the dug-up area. By this time, the female is exhausted and will want to rest and drink.

Moving Eggs
Remove loose dirt from the eggs with a soft paintbrush, and gently mark the top of each egg with a pencil. As the embryo starts to develop, it orients itself right side up, so it is important to know where the "top" is. Rotating the egg during incubation can slow development, and in some cases, kill the embryo. As you remove the eggs, gently place them in an egg carton or in damp vermiculite for transport to the incubator. If you should accidentally roll or turn an egg during the process, little harm is done, as the embryo at this point in time consists of a small number of cells and is not yet oriented.

Egg Incubation

A Few Words About Turtle Eggs
Turtle eggs have a shell composed of calcium. The shell is porous; oxygen and moisture are taken in, carbon dioxide and other gases pass out of the egg during the embryo's development. For this reason, eggs should not be incubated in a sealed container, to avoid oxygen depletion and a buildup of toxic gases.

The turtle embryo develops within the amniotic sac, which is attached to the inside wall of the egg. The sac can be ruptured or torn from the wall of the egg if handled too roughly, which is why handling the eggs is not recommended during development. The eggs should not be turned, either - once development begins, the embryo orients itself right side up. Turning the egg can slow development, damage tissues and tiny blood vessels, or in some cases, kill the embryo. Freshly laid eggs can be picked up and turned if necessary, since the embryo consists of just a few cells and is not yet oriented, but take care and err on the side of caution. It is recommended that the eggs be marked on the top with a pencil, and care taken not to disturb them during incubation.

Eggs can discolor during incubation, but this does not necessarily mean the egg is infertile or has spoiled. Occasionally, a fungal infection will appear on the surface of the shell, and again, this is not always an indicator of infertility. Fungus is more prevalent in high humidity. You can isolate any infected eggs to prevent the fungus from spreading to other eggs.

Incubation Media, Egg Placement and Containment
Vermiculite is the substrate used by most tortoise keepers to keep developing eggs on. It retains moisture, and distributes it evenly. Typically, vermiculite and water are mixed together in a 1:1 ratio by weight, producing damp, but not wet, vermiculite. I generally add enough water to soak it thoroughly, then squeeze out the excess water by making a fist, which achieves about the same result. The eggs should not be buried, but placed in shallow depressions over several inches of medium. Use a thumb or a spoon to press in shallow indentations for each egg. These will help to hold the egg in place.

Other substrates such as Pearlite® or vermiculite mixed with sphagnum moss and sand are used, but plain vermiculite and water is by far the most popular method. The moisture level should be checked regularly during the incubation period.

The eggs and substrate should be placed in a container with a lid to keep the humidity stable. Plastic food containers work well, as do plastic seed germinators. The lid should preferably be transparent, and should remove easily without the risk of shaking the container. A few small holes should be punched in the container or in the lid to allow for air exchange.

Temperature and Humidity
There is a narrow range of temperature and humidity at which Redfoot eggs will develop properly. Too low, and the embryo will not develop; high temperatures or humidity levels at or close to 100 per cent will kill the embryo.

Lowman (1996) incubates Redfoot eggs at 84°F (29°C) with the humidity between 70% and 80%, using water and vermiculite mixed together in equal weights. Zimmerman (1995) recommends incubating at 86F (30°C) with 80% humidity. Highfield (1996) suggests 86 °F with "moderately high humidity". A drop of a few degrees at night is not harmful and may actually be beneficial, and is certainly more akin to what tortoise eggs go through in the wild.

Incubation periods can range from 120 to 175 days, with the average is around 150 days. As an example, Iris, my adult female, laid her first clutch of eggs on July 4th, and they hatched 147 days later on November 28th. Warmer temperatures can reduce the incubation period somewhat, but this is not always the case.

For many species of tortoises, incubation temperatures can determine gender. Lower temperatures within the range predominantly produce males, while higher temperatures produce females. For Redfoot tortoises, Highfield (1996) indicates that 32°C (89.6°F) will produce mostly females, while 27.5°C (81.5°F) and below produces mainly males. Incubation temperatures midway between these two figures should produce a mix of genders.

Handling and Candling
As stated elsewhere in this book, turtle eggs should be handled as little as possible, if at all. However, you may wish to candle the eggs several weeks after

they are laid, to determine whether they are fertile. This can be carefully done without disturbing the eggs. A pocket flashlight with a small diameter can be used for candling. In a darkened room, place the flashlight up against the side of the egg; this should illuminate the egg enough to see some detail inside. A fertile egg will have blood vessels forming on the inside shell walls, and in older eggs the embryo mass can be visible. This is not an entirely fool-proof method - sometimes you cannot tell whether the egg is fertile or not. Keep the egg, even if you can't see anything. Of course, foul-smelling or cracked eggs should be removed.

Incubators
There are a number of simple incubators that can be purchased or constructed fairly easily. Some of the most popular methods are discussed here. Maintaining proper temperature and humidity ranges is the primary function of any incubator. As it is for maintaining a proper enclosure, a good electronic thermometer is essential for successful egg incubation. Proper temperature ranges within the incubator should be established before any eggs are laid. Make sure you purchase a unit that records high and low temperatures in memory, invaluable for testing a full 24 hour cycle. An electronic unit featuring both a thermometer and hydrometer for measuring humidity makes monitoring even easier. Incubators should be placed somewhere safe from accidental bumping or other disturbances.

The Warm Room Technique
If you have a reptile room or some other room with stable temperatures within the range needed for incubation, you can simply place the egg container in a safe, out-of-the-way spot within the room. For example, I have a friend who incubates eggs in a closet containing a hot water heater. The egg container is placed on a shelf above the water heater, where the temperature stays near 84 degrees (29°C) during the day, and a few degrees cooler at night. Such a closet is fairly stable in a home where the climate is thermostatically controlled.

The Immersion Incubator
This incubator works well for eggs requiring fairly high humidity. Components include a watertight Styrofoam box with a lid, a submersible aquarium heater (not the hang-on-the-side type), and some bricks. Water is added to the box, enough to cover the heater by several inches. The bricks are used to make a platform to suspend the egg container several inches above the waterline. Using an electronic thermometer, the submersible heater is adjusted to the proper temperature, and the unit is tested empty for several days to ensure that the unit functions properly. Drawbacks: A cheap heater can malfunction and either overheats or does not heat at all. Spend a little more money and get a high quality unit. A second thermometer can be added as a backup in case of failure, and set to a degree or two lower. Water levels should be monitored closely. An aquarium can be substituted for a Styrofoam box, and sheets of Styrofoam can be cut and taped around the bottom and sides to help keep the temperature stable.

The Dry Heat Incubator
Similar to the Immersion Incubator. Components include a lidless Styrofoam or wooden box, a human heating pad, an electronic thermostat, bricks and hardware cloth. The box should be deep enough so that the egg container is at least several

inches below the top. The heating pad is placed on the box bottom, and is connected to the electronic thermostat. The hardware cloth is cut to fit inside the box, and the bricks are used to hold the hardware cloth up several inches above the pad (no bricks should be placed on the pad), and the egg container is placed on the hardware cloth. Bricks help to add weight and stability to the set-up. The thermostat is adjusted, and the unit is operated empty for several days to test. Drawbacks: With this dry incubator, humidity levels within the egg container must be closely monitored.

Chick Incubators
Hovabator® and other brands of chick incubators can be purchased at farm supply stores. They usually feature a Styrofoam box and lid, with a heating element and thermostat built into the lid. There are reservoirs in the bottom designed to hold water and thus keep the humidity levels up. They are simple to set up and cost around $30 US. Drawbacks: The mechanical thermostats are not always reliable. Humidity levels must be closely monitored, since these devices can quickly dry out incubation media. Some tortoise keepers report good results using them, others have had problems and no longer use chick incubators.

Caring For Hatchlings

After months of development (and anxious waiting on your part) the baby tortoises are ready to leave the egg. They scratch and break through the shell with the aid of an egg tooth, a tiny triangular appendage attached to the upper beak. Once the shell has been pierced, the hatchling may bite away pieces of shell or push with its front legs to enlarge the opening. It is not unusual for hatchlings to remain inside the shell for several days, resting and gaining strength while they absorb nutrients from their yolk sac, which is attached underneath through the plastron. The yolk sac provides nutrients to the hatchlings as they struggle out of the egg and then up to the surface, no small task indeed! The yolk sac distorts the plastron somewhat, but after absorption the plates come together in normal fashion. The egg tooth falls off after a number of days.

Often, and for reasons not well understood, the hatching of the first egg can trigger the others to hatch. Now it is time to watch the eggs carefully. Sometimes a hatchling will pierce the shell, but is too weak to break out of the egg completely. If you notice a neonate struggling to break out without success after several hours, you can provide some assistance. A small pair of tweezers can be used to break away bits of shell and enlarge the opening a little. Continue to watch over several hours for progress, and enlarge the opening further if necessary. Another problem hatchlings can have is becoming glued to the shell by the albumen and other egg liquids as they dry. Carefully and patiently, use wet cotton-tipped applicators to remove the substance.

The Neonate Nursery
Once a hatchling leaves the egg, it should be removed to a previously prepared container serving as a nursery. The nursery should maintain the same humidity and temperature that the eggs were incubated at, with a lid to maintain temperature and humidity levels. It can be as simple as a plastic sweater box with slightly damp paper towels as a substrate.

The neonates should remain under observation in the nursery for a week or more while they absorb their yolk sacs. The yolk sac is an opening into the body of the neonate, so the nursery needs to be kept as clean as possible to prevent infections. The damp paper towels help prevent the yolk sac from adhering to the floor of the nursery container, and should be changed at least daily. The eggshells should be placed in the nursery after wiping any substrate particles off; the hatchlings will eat pieces of the shell and may have developmental problems if not provided with this initial intake of calcium. It may be several days before the neonates develop an interest in food.

The Hatchling Enclosure

Once they are eating, and the yolk sac has been absorbed and the plastron has closed up, it is time for the little Redfoot tortoises to leave the nursery for their everyday enclosure. From this point on, they need the same requirements of light, heat, diet, etc., that adults need. Their enclosure should be furnished with hide boxes, water dishes, and small stones and sticks and other interesting things to climb over and investigate, but nothing that might cause them to fall or turn upside down. They should not be kept with larger tortoises, and they should be handled gently. Keep in mind that small turtles have very little mass and can overheat and cool down far more rapidly than adults.

Many keepers also add a layer of damp sphagnum moss to the inside of the hide house, in order to provide an area with higher humidity, useful when keeping Redfoot tortoises where it is difficult to maintain 60-80 per cent humidity levels.

Some keepers use a soil-sand-peat mixture as a substrate, which I have tried and it seems to work well. After the young tortoises gain some size, I use a fine grade of cypress mulch, slightly dampened, and a layer of dried leaves, which adds some security. Hatchlings in the wild spend their first few years hidden in the leaf litter and dried grasses.

Final Considerations

Things to remember

- Small turtles have very little mass and will overheat or chill rapidly.
- Tortoises are faster than you think; never leave them unattended in open areas.
- Redfoot tortoises and other turtles will bulldoze right under a chain link fence.
- Your tortoise won't starve if it misses a meal!

Things to consider

- Do you have a plan if there is a power outage?
- Who will take care of your Redfoot tortoises when you are sick, on vacation, etc.?
- Who will receive your long-lived tortoises should you pass away?
- Do you have a good veterinarian?

- Keep regular records of growth - weight, length, etc. Take notes during any health problems or unusual behavior.

Things to avoid

- Ivermectin
- Hot rocks
- Spinach
- Turning your turtle upside down unless absolutely necessary (they don't like it, and many species have trouble breathing easily when upside down). Don't stress your pet this way if it isn't necessary.
- Turning turtle eggs - remember, the embryo's amniotic sac is attached to the shell!

References and Resources

The Practical Encyclopedia of Keeping and Breeding Tortoises and Freshwater Turtles by A.C. Highfield. Carapace Press, 1996. 295 pp. ISBN: 1-873943-06-7
The Captive Maintenance and Propagation of the Red-Footed and Yellow-Footed Tortoises by Rodney J. Lowman. Reptiles Magazine, December 1996.
The Complete Idiot's Guide to Turtles and Tortoises by Liz Palika. Alpha Books, 1998. 270 pp. ISBN: 0-87605-143-3
The Consumer's Guide to Feeding Reptiles by Liz Palika. Simon and Schuster, 1997. 136 pp. ISBN: 0-87605-681-8
Encyclopedia of Turtles by Dr. Peter Pritchard. TFH Publications, 1979. 895 pp. ISBN: 0-87666-918-6
The Great Redfoot Tortoise by Richard Cary Paull. Green Nature Books, 1997. 115 pp. ISBN: 1-888089-37-7
Disease Prevention in Tortoise Collections by A. C. Highfield. Tortoise Trust Article. Available on web: www.tortoisetrust.org
The Official Tortoise Trust Guide to Tortoises and Turtles by A. C. Highfield. Carapace Press, 1994. ISBN: 1-873943-01-6
Reptiles and Amphibians: Care, Behavior, and Reproduction by Elke Zimmerman. TFH Publications, 1995. 384 pp. ISBN: 0-86622-541-2
The South American Herpetofauna: Its Origin, Evolution, and Dispersal edited by William E. Duellman. University of Kansas Museum of Natural History Monograph No. 7, 1979. 485 pp. ISBN: 0-89338-008-3
Small Animal Clinical Nutrition III by Lewis, Morris, and Hand. Mark Morris Associates, 1987.
Terrarium and Cage Construction and Care by Richard and Patricia Bartlett. Barron's, 1999. 217 pp. ISBN: 0-7641-0673-2
The Turtle Table by David Kirkpatrick. Reptile & Amphibian Magazine, July/Aug. 1990, pg 16-19.
The Tortoise & Turtle Feeding Manual by A. C. Highfield, Carapace Press, 2000. 52 pp. ISBN: 1-873943-23-7
Turtles, Tortoises, and Terrapins by Fritz Jurgen Obst. St. Martins, 1988. 231 pp. ISBN: 0-312-82362-2

Turtles of the World by Carl H. Ernst and Roger W. Barbour. Smithsonian Press, 1989. 313 pp. ISBN: 1-56098-212-8
Turtles and Tortoises - A Complete Owner's Manual by Richard and Patricia Bartlett. Barron's, 1996. 119 pp. ISBN: 0-8120-9712-2

Web Sites

www.tortoisetrust.org - The Tortoise Trust
www.tortoise.org - California Turtle and Tortoise Club (CTTC)
www.ttmasterclass.com - Courses and seminars for tortoise and turtle keepers
www.ttinstitute.net - Online and distance education programs for tortoise and turtle keepers. This site offers the excellent 'Tortoise Trust Foundation Course in Chelonian Husbandry'.
www.carapacepress.com - Specialist publisher of tortoise and turtle titles.

Glossary

abdominal scutes The third rearmost pair of scutes on the plastron. The abdominal scutes are usually located centrally between the front and rear sets of legs, and are normally the largest scutes on the plastron.
anal scutes The rearmost pair of scutes on the plastron. Anal scutes are often different shapes for males and females.
annuli Growth rings apparent on the scutes of tortoises and other kinds of turtles.
anterior Toward the head.
axillary scutes On the plastron, the scutes located at the anterior ends of the bridge, just posterior to where the front legs emerge.
basking The process by which turtles and other reptiles obtain and regulate heat using the warmth of the sun. Basking is an important element in the daily routine of most cold-blooded reptiles. See **ectothermic, thermoregulation**.
beak The horny sheaths covering the upper and lower jaws; also refers to the jaws in general.
bridge The part of the shell on either side of the turtle that connects the plastron and the carapace.
brumation The winter dormancy period of amphibians and reptiles.
carapace The top shell.
caudal Pertaining to the tail.
central scutes The large scutes extending down the midline of the carapace, usually five in number.
chelonians Turtles and tortoises.
cloaca The chamber just inside the anal opening. The urinary and digestive tracts end here, as does the reproductive tract; urine, feces, and eggs are expelled from the cloaca's single opening.
costals The large scutes running down the carapace, on either side of the central scutes, usually four in number. Also referred to as lateral scutes.
crepuscular Active at dusk or dawn.
diurnal Active during the day.
ectothermic Cold-blooded. Ectotherms cannot regulate their body temperature and are at the mercy of their environment. See **thermoregulation, basking**.

estivation A summer period of dormancy similar to brumation, where activity and metabolism slow down during periods of extreme heat or drought. The animal typically retires to a burrow or some other means of shelter.
femoral scutes The pair of scutes behind the abdominal scutes and in front of the anal scutes on the plastron, usually in line with the back legs.
gestation The time of embryo development, between egg fertilization and egg laying.
gravid Pregnant.
gular scutes The frontmost pair of scutes on the plastron. Occasionally there is a single gular scute.
hibernation see **brumation**.
humeral scutes The second pair of scutes on the plastron, behind the gular scutes.
inguinal scutes On the plastron, scutes located on the posterior ends of the bridge, right in front of where the hind legs emerge.
keratin The horn-like protein comprising the scutes, beaks, and claws.
lamina, laminae Another term for scutes.
marginal scutes The small scutes around the edge of the carapace.
nocturnal Active at night..
oviposition The laying of eggs.
ovipositor A soft, tubular structure that extends from the vent during egg-laying. The ovipositor helps the eggs fall a shorter distance into the excavated nest cavity.
pectoral scutes The pair of scutes just in front of the abdominal scutes on the plastron.
plastron The bottom shell.
posterior Towards the rear or tail.
seam The line of contact between scutes.
scutes The horny plates covering the bones of both the plastron and carapace. Also called laminae, scutes are composed of keratin.
suture The jagged connection between two shell bones.
thermoregulation Control of body temperatures in cold-blooded animals; when too cold, they seek warmer temperatures, when too warm, they seek colder temperatures. See **basking, ectothermic**
tympanum The surface that forms the external ear in turtles; the 'ear drum'.
vent The outside opening of the cloaca.

Acknowledgements

Thanks go out to all the tortoise people I've talked to in the course of this project. Tortoise keepers are a special breed - they're warm, caring, compassionate and passionate people, every one. Special thanks to Nada Cagle, Carol Cox and Susan Brummit for sharing their personal insights, Redfoot information and care experiences. Andy Highfield and others at The Tortoise Trust looked over this manuscript. I am in their debt. To my wife, Nell, for putting up with all of the long hours I've spent hunched over tortoises and computer keyboards, and the volumes of odd fruit and vegetables crammed into the refrigerator - thank you, dear.

Other publications from Carapace Press

PRACTICAL CARE OF RUSSIAN TORTOISES
Comprehensive data on the care of Russian, or Steppe tortoises (*Testudo horsfieldii*) presented in the form of an informative video with accompanying manual. Covers habitat requirements, dietary management, identification, sexing, hibernation and general care. The habitat construction section is particularly informative, and covers keeping Russian tortoises in both indoor and outdoor enclosures.

PRACTICAL CARE OF LEOPARD AND SULCATA TORTOISES
Comprehensive data on the care of these two large species with similar captive maintenance requirements, presented in the form of an informative video with accompanying manual. Covers habitat requirements, dietary management, identification, sexing and general care. Heating and lighting is covered in depth, and some excellent ideas are presented on how to provide summer and winter housing.

PRACTICAL CARE OF MEDITERRANEAN (GREEK) TORTOISES
Highly detailed information on the care and maintenance of *Testudo* species. Identification, design of near-natural accommodation, feeding and breeding. Informative video with comprehensive accompanying book.

PRACTICAL CARE OF RED-EARED SLIDERS AND PAINTED TURTLES
A detailed video and book combination revealing exactly how to set up and maintain these popular species successfully. Pond and tank design, filtration, heating and lighting etc., are all covered extensively.

www.carapacepress.com

New Course in Tortoise & Turtle Husbandry

The vast majority of problems affecting tortoises in captivity arise because so few keepers fully understand the basic biology and real needs of these highly specialized animals. In addition, many 'pet care' books are full of inaccurate and misleading (sometimes lethal) advice. The Tortoise Trust publishes a wide range of excellent quality care sheets and other articles, many of which are available on-line free of charge at our website. However, there is no substitute for taking part in a carefully designed and highly structured learning program, where you can learn about tortoises and their care using a logical, step-by-step approach, and where your progress is monitored to ensure that you fully understand everything.

The **Tortoise Trust Foundation Course in Chelonian Husbandry** is now available for you to study in your own home, either on-line or via post. This is a truly excellent and comprehensive introduction to this subject. Whether you are a beginner or more experienced keeper, we guarantee that this course will prove invaluable and fascinating! In addition to the **Foundation Course** several **Advanced Modules** will also be available shortly, covering such areas as reproductive biology, advanced care of aquatic species, and veterinary management.

The Foundation Course includes:

- ❑ Basic tortoise and turtle biology
- ❑ Behavior
- ❑ Temperate and Tropical species care
- ❑ Care of aquatic and semi-terrestrial species
- ❑ Heating and lighting requirements
- ❑ Hibernation management
- ❑ Designing accommodation
- ❑ Dietary management
- ❑ Disease prevention and detection

Produced and fully endorsed by the world-famous TORTOISE TRUST, leaders in education for tortoise and turtle keepers worldwide

www.ttinstitute.net